THE
CAT DAY
BOOK

First published in 2003 by
Michael O'Mara Books Limited
9 Lion Yard, Tremadoc Road,
London SW4 7NQ

ISBN 1-84317-022-1

3 5 7 9 10 8 6 4 2

Designed by Design 23

Origination by Colourwise Ltd

Printed and bound by Eurolitho SpA, Milan

THE
CAT DAY
BOOK

Mighty Mouth

Mimi tries to look scary.

INTRODUCTION

If the dog is man's best friend, what does that make the cat? As George Mikes wrote in *How To Be Decadent*: 'You can keep a dog; but it is the cat who keeps people, because cats find humans useful domestic animals.' Even the most biased cat lover would admit that cats shed hair on everything, give us allergic reactions, are ferocious killers (given the chance), fight under our beds in the early morning, and generally do as they please. Yet they have only to sit beside us and purr and our hearts melt.

Cats were part of daily life in Egypt about 5,000 years ago. They were used to hunt fish and birds, as well as to kill the rodents in the grain stores. The pharaohs considered cats so valuable that they were protected by law. After an Egyptian cat died, its body was mummified. One cemetery found in the nineteenth century contained over 300,000 mummified cats. The goddess Bastet was always shown with the head of a cat, and many images of her have survived.

Incidentally, the ancient Egyptians found a mystical quality in a cat's purr. One medicinal text stated that a purring cat could induce a more restful and tranquil sleep. In modern times, it has been scientifically proven that owning cats is good for our health and can reduce high blood pressure and other illnesses.

Most of our modern breeds are descended from these ancient cats. Domestic cats bred freely as they spread across the world. As a result, cats have evolved in an incredible variety of sizes, shapes and colours. Several breeds first appeared in Asia, including the Burmese and Siamese. The Persian cat was bred in ancient Persia (now Iran). But domestic cats never reached North America – the first cats came with early European colonists. The thirty-six recognized breeds of pedigree cats can be grouped into two general categories: the long-haired Persian, and the domestic shorthair.

Brown-striped and blotched cats most closely resemble their wild ancestors. Tabby patterns occur in various colours, including red (orange), cream, blue (grey), brown, silver and smoke. Solid white is the rarest colour for a moggy, while solid black or blue are relatively rare. Almost all solid blacks have a few white hairs. Black-and-orange cats are known as tortoiseshells, and tricolours or calicoes when white is also present.

Cats have much more sensitive hearing than humans or dogs. They see six times better in the dark than humans do. There are around 60,000 hairs per square inch on a cat's back and double that on its underside. On average, a cat will sleep for sixteen hours a day, but they can run at up to thirty miles per hour when necessary.

This superb collection of cats and kittens, in all kinds of situations from the hilarious to the touching, will be a real tonic for anyone feeling down or tired. You will wonder at the skill and patience of the photographers who have produced such a magnificent portfolio of felines for your enjoyment. Throughout this book, and often in the same picture, tenderness and (cat) dignity rub shoulders with the comic and the quirky. Even in the most extreme conditions, these enchanting cats never lose their cool. And for those sourpusses who don't like cats, just consider your aversion probably stems from being a mouse in a previous existence!

Crown Prince

William finds it exhausting practising for the day he will be King.

The Eyes Have It

Only one of these kittens knows that it's rude to stare.

Commercial Break

This was the biggest fish bowl
Ginger had ever seen.

Yee Haa!

Take your partner in the hand,
along the arm, on the head…

Pulling a Pint

Blackie and Brownie
loved milking time.

The Cat On the Hat

Snowy Far has company while collecting for the blind.

Cooped Up

Kitty rather enjoys being henned in.

The Meow-sic Room

Mitzi has studied for three years and is a virtuoso performer.

Ebony and Ivory

Tabitha has the key to playing the piano.

Make It Snappy

A right couple of posers.

Music, Tweet Music

Tosca and Twitter know the score
when owner Stan Albertson takes to
the organ.

Peek-a-Bow!

Clara looks a picture at the
New York Empire Cat Show.

Cat Caught on Canvas

Gjon Mili's cat, Blackie, assesses his
portrait by Saul Steinberg.

Have Cat, Will Travel

Buster the cat with owner Max Corkill on a 1952
Deluxe Sunbeam. Buster has travelled over
250,000 kilometres on the road.

Pond Life

Curiosity could well kill the fish.

Queen of Sheba

Mussy, the Turkish Van cat, is a delight in her jewels.

The Perch

Benny won't budge from his favourite bagpuss.

Cocktail Hour at the Savoy

Whisky, the Lloyds mouser, sits on the shoulder of yeoman Nobby Clark at a
launch party in 1953 for the book *Cockney Cats*, by Warren Tute.

Close Encounter I

Close Encounter II

Stop mousing around!

A tasty mousel,
do you not think?

Mouse Guest

Not today, thank you.

Headhunter

Jinx clearly doesn't think much of his white fur hat.

Get My Drift?

Fluffy is determined not to get her paws wet.

Harbouring a Grudge

A Greek pelican administers a catnip.

Meat and No Veg

A street butcher feeds his customers at
the turn of the twentieth century.

Eight-paw Beat

Teddy and Polly sing from the same hymn sheet.

Bear Essentials

Vodka and Ice model the latest must-have accessory.

All For One

The Three Mouseketeers – Porthos, Athos and Aramis.

A Prickly Situation

Spike and Mike don't always see eye-to-eye.

Sun Lounger

Ronnie gets some rays.

Doormat

These mice will soon have the rug pulled out from under them.

Chimp and Zee

Zee tells his good pal Chimp that he looks a chump in his outfit.

Log Jam

The quick black cat jumps on to the lazy fox.

Cat and Mouse I

Cat and Mouse II

Frank has become an Internet
celebrity, recovering from a
road accident live on the web.

Sammy can't get a squeak
out of this mouse.

Bareback Rider

Sooty jockeys for position.

The Tortoise and the Pair

Minnie and Mickey join Thomas in the slow lane.

Pint-size

Tiggy hits the bottle again.

Acting Up

Actress Kim Novak playing with Siamese cats which performed with her in the 1958 film, *Bell, Book and Candle*.

Mice Work If You Can Get It

Tom's thrilled to see it's raining mice.

Rugby Tackle

Prop the bulldog is tackled to the ground by Fly Half.

Bird's-eye View

Kelly Kitten listens patiently to Simon Sparrow's complaints.

Driving Miss Daisy

Bertie the bulldog borrows his master's toy car to chauffeur his mistress.

Black and White

Darling, we were made for each other.

A Fine Ass-pect

'Ears looking at you, kit'.

Trunk Call

Nelly ferries her feline friend.

Stairway to Heaven

Three moggies take steps to make themselves comfortable.

The Draughtsmen

Larry Lamb and Percy Pussy enjoy a game under the
watchful eye of Colin Cockerel.

Bubble Trouble

What happens next?

Cold Feet

Poppy gives herself a pedicure.

The Big Bang

Now you see it...

...now you don't.

A Late Booking

Byron browses a book before bedtime.

For Whom the Cat Toils

This feline knows the importance of being Ernest Hemingway's cat (1955).

Testing, Testing …

Tiger takes time out from his mouse-catching job
at Lockheed's Test Facility.

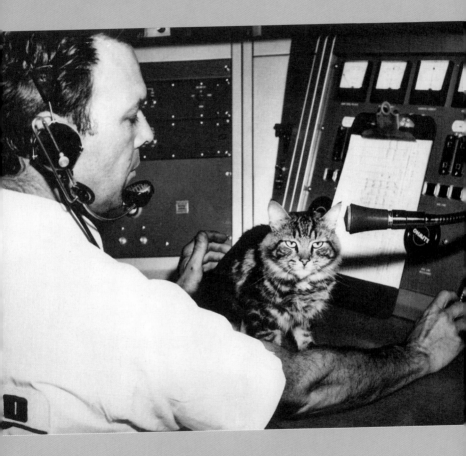

Seeing Double

Bunny coincidence.

Little Black Numbers

Owners wait in line to audition their cats for a
role in the 1961 movie, *Tales of Terror*.

The Season of Goodwill

A kitten is not just for Christmas.

Keep a Lid On It

Suki can't stand the competition.

Beach Bums

Three hungry cats wait for their breakfast on Moorea Island.

Water Baby

Custard goes for two fifteen-minute swimming sessions a week. His favourite stroke is the doggy paddle.

Golden Slumbers

Snowy wisely lets sleeping
dogs lie.

Catlick

Mum makes sure Baby's clean
behind the ears.

Paw-trait of the Artist

Pablo brushes up on his pawstrokes.

PHOTO CREDITS